Unicorn
Libro da colorare

Coloring Pages for Kids

Coloring Pages for Kids
An imprint of Ciparum LLC

Unicorn libro da colorare
© 2017 Ciparum LLC
All rights reserved.
ISBN-10:1-63589-428-X
ISBN-13:978-1-63589-428-8

Coloring Pages for Kids

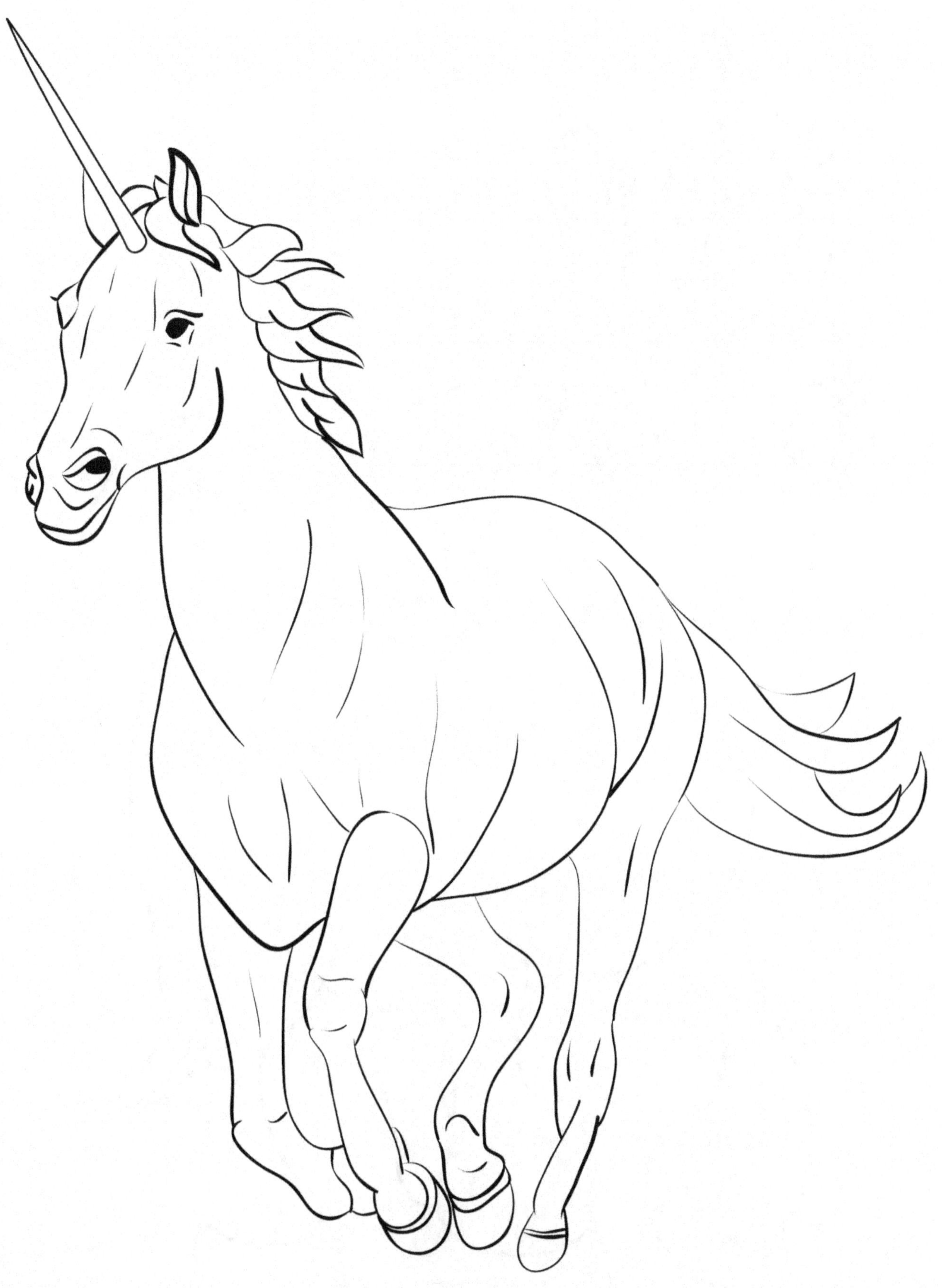

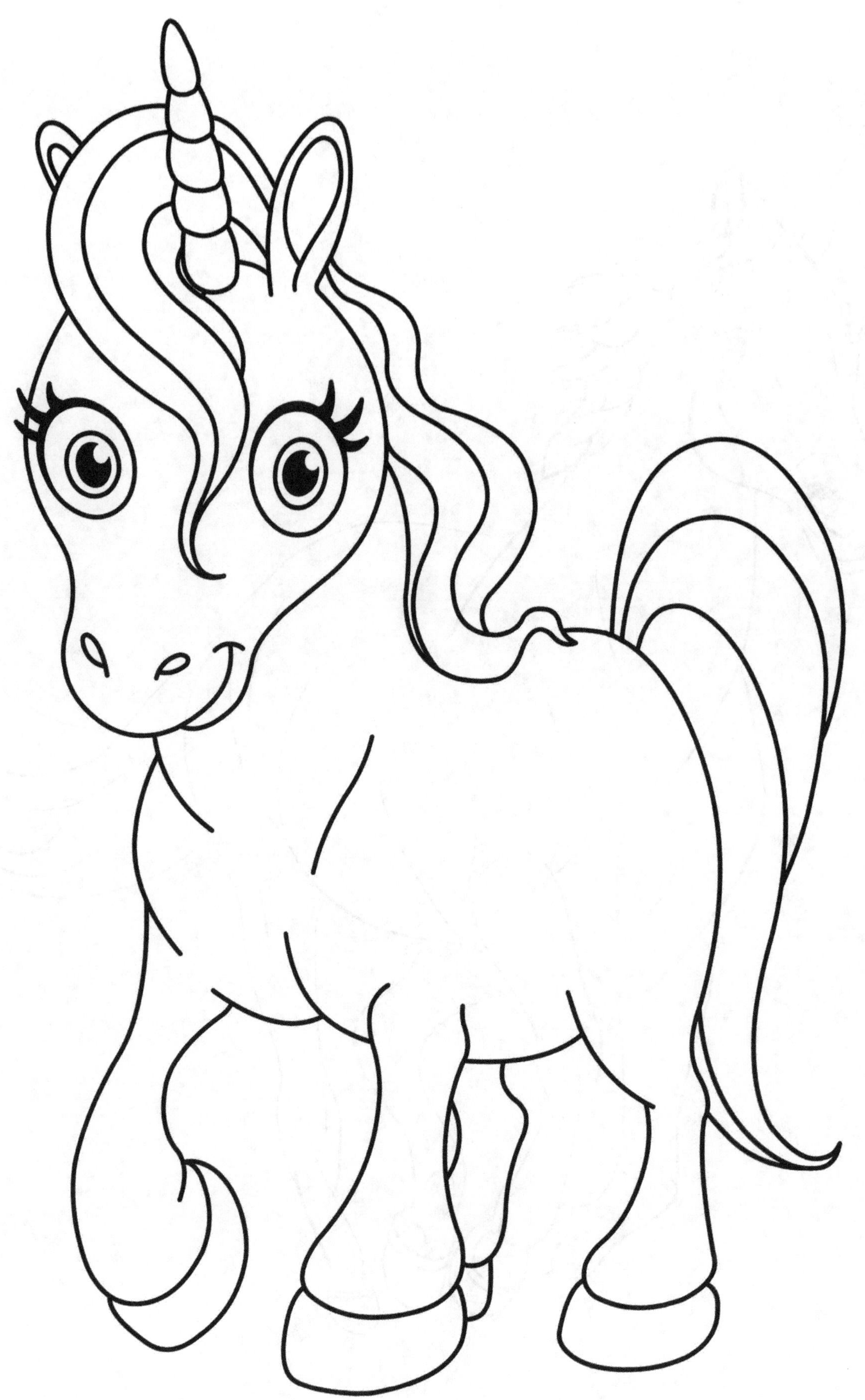

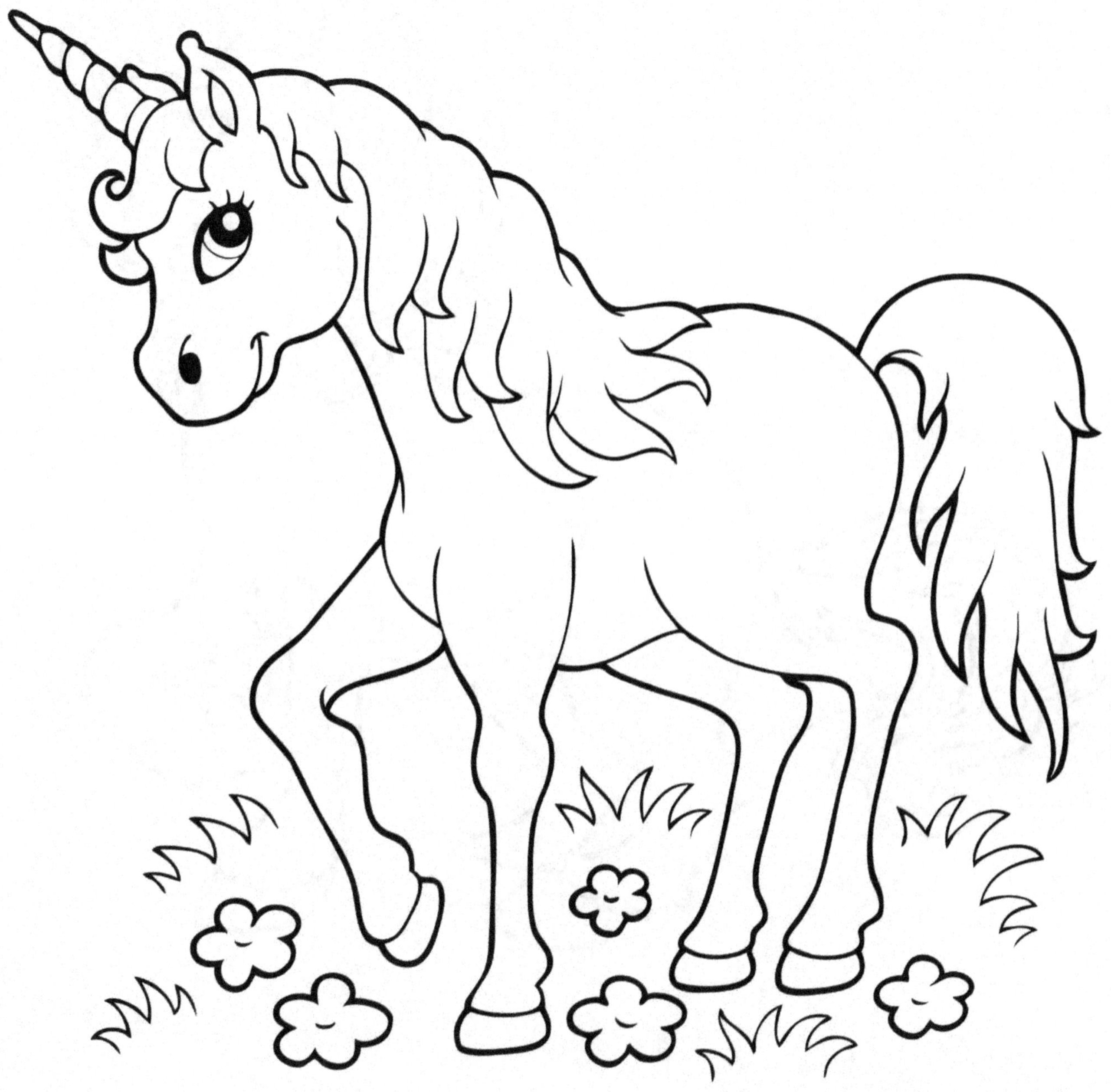

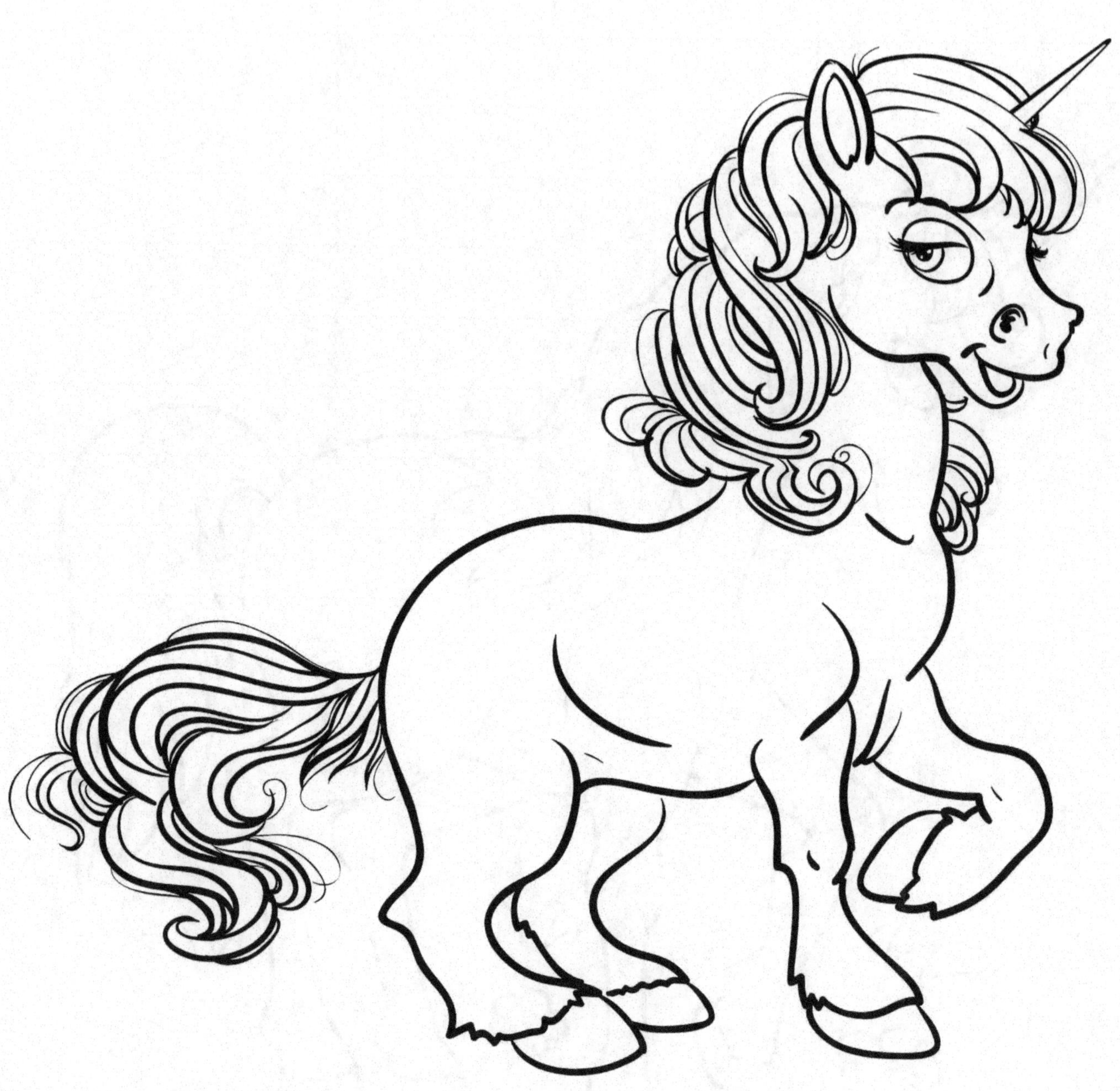

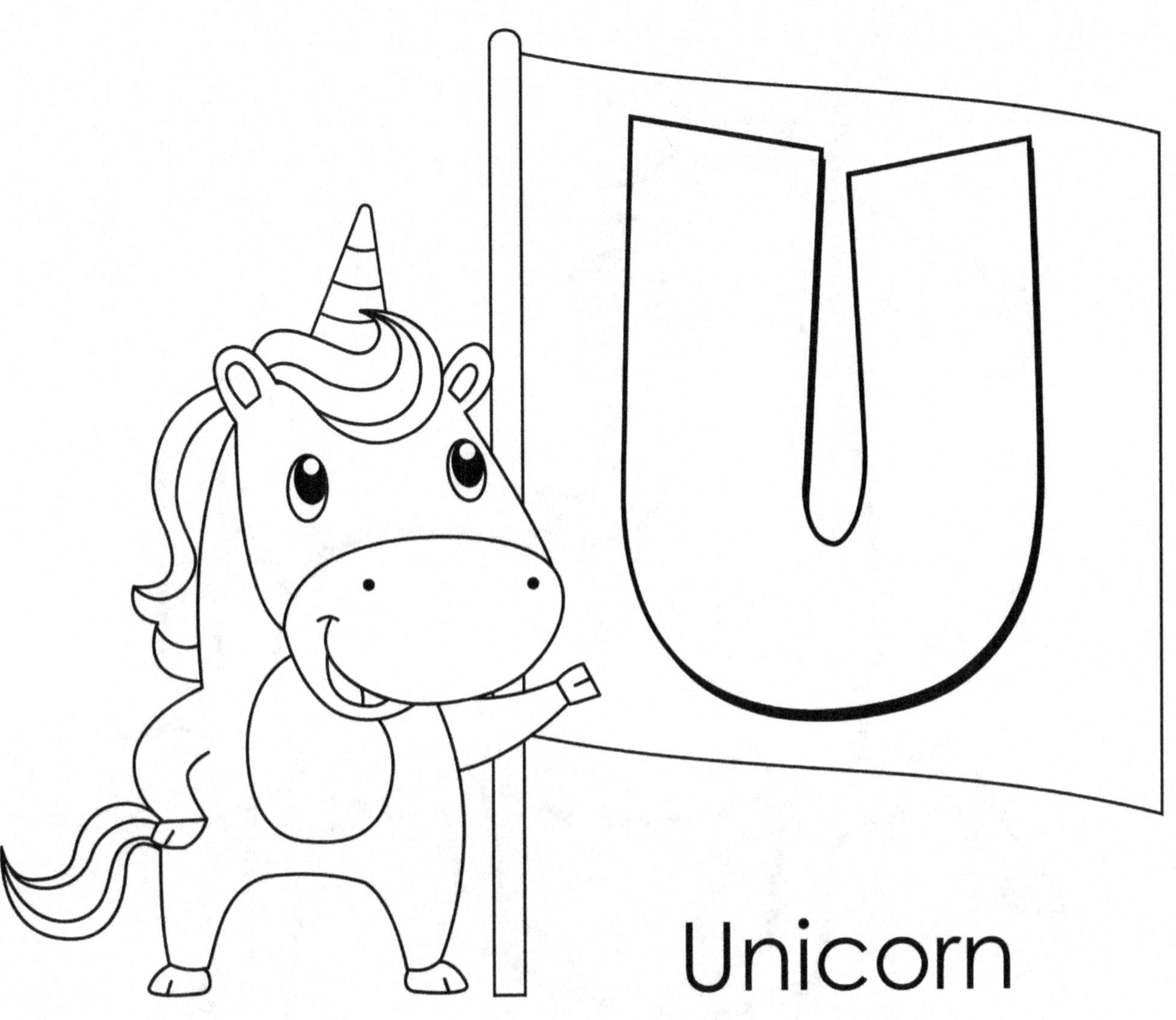

Unicorn

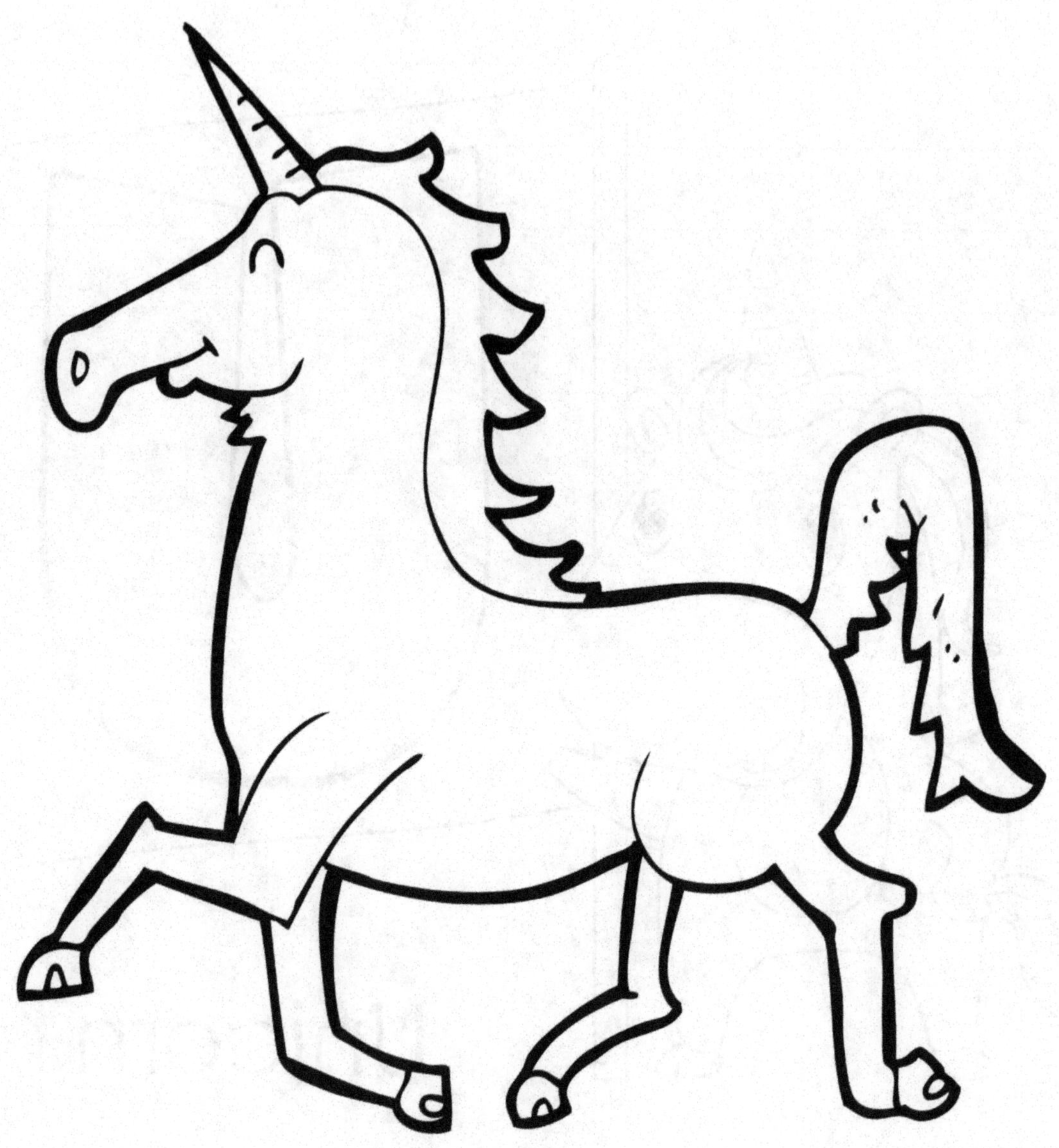

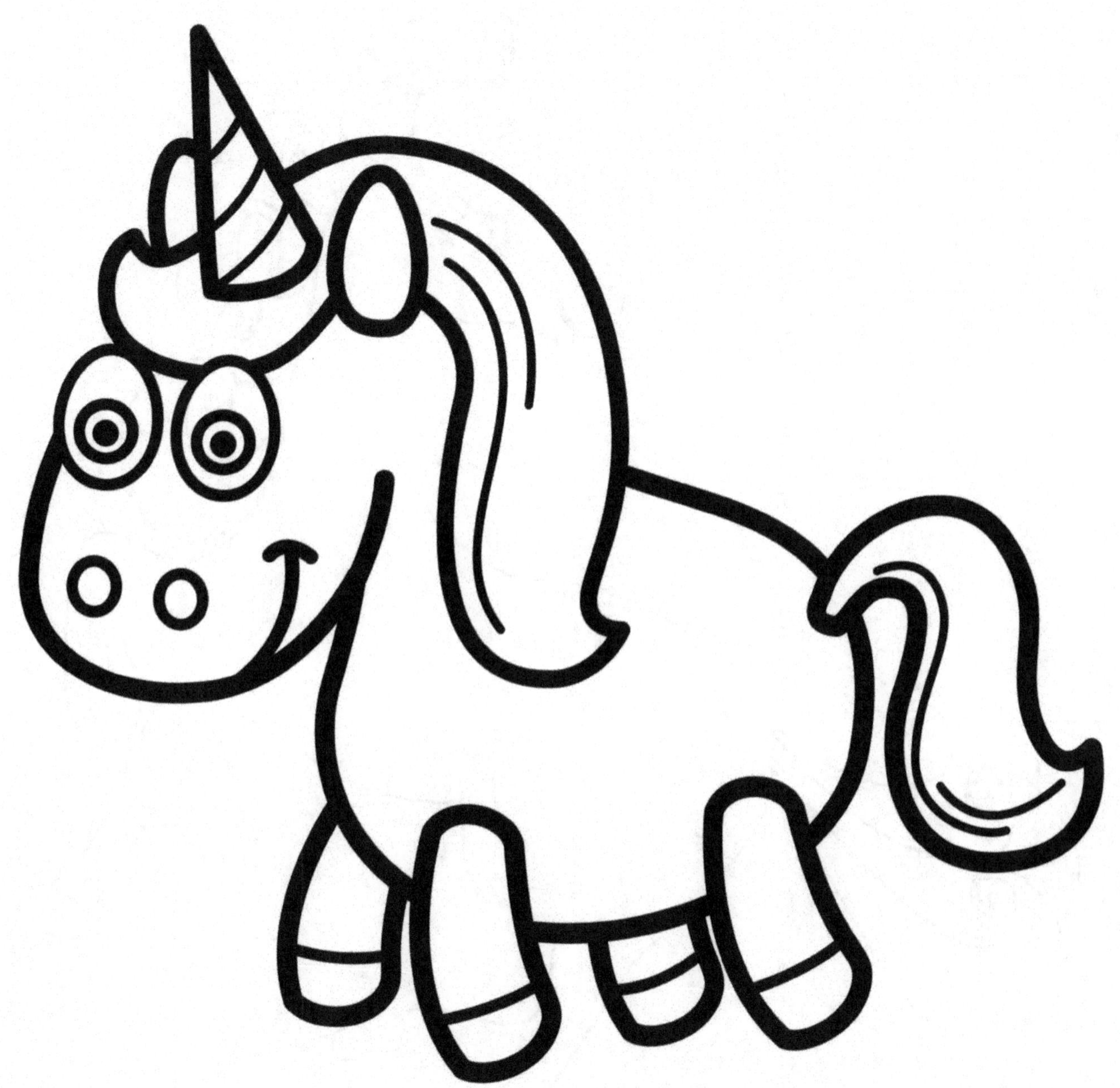

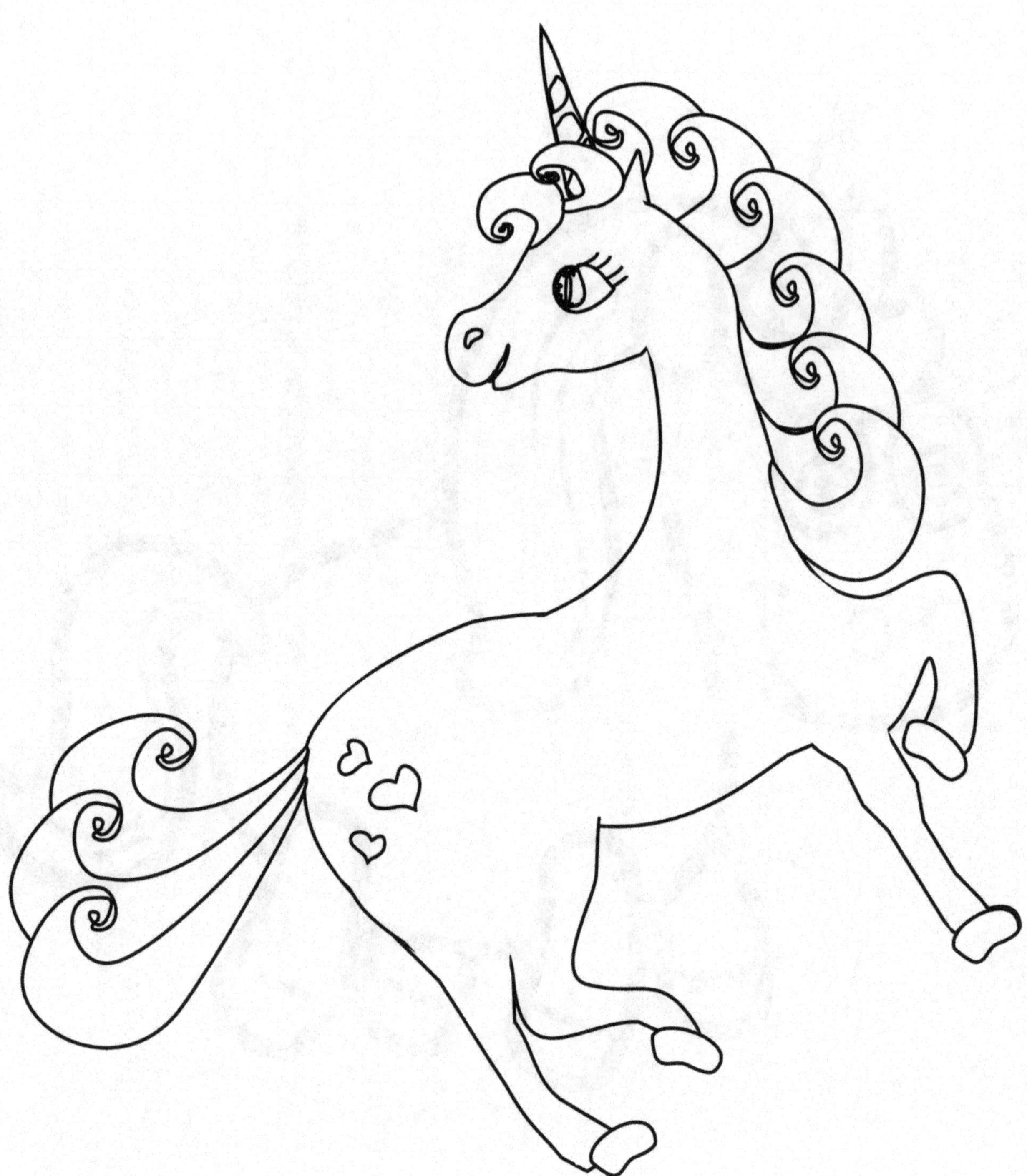

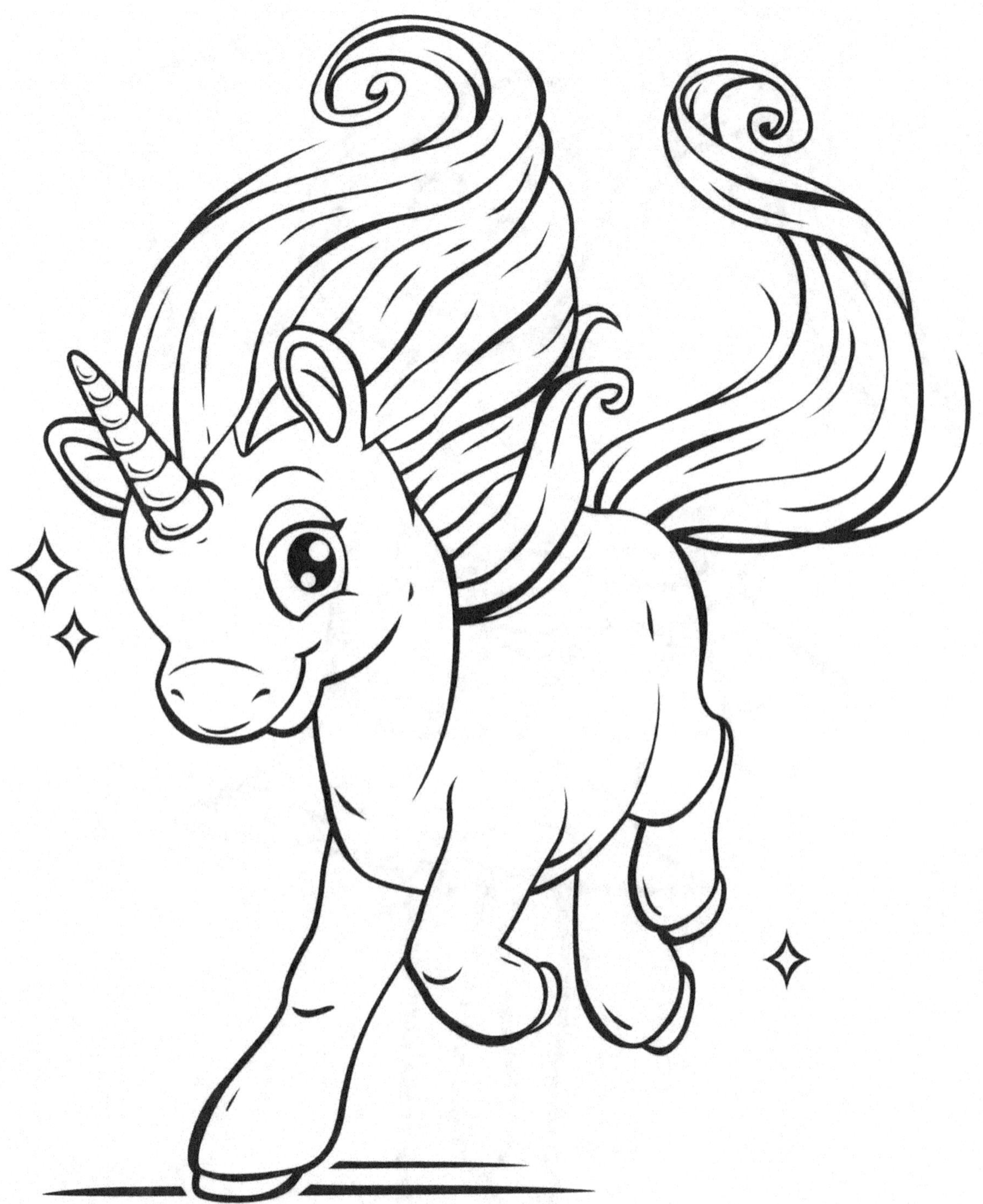

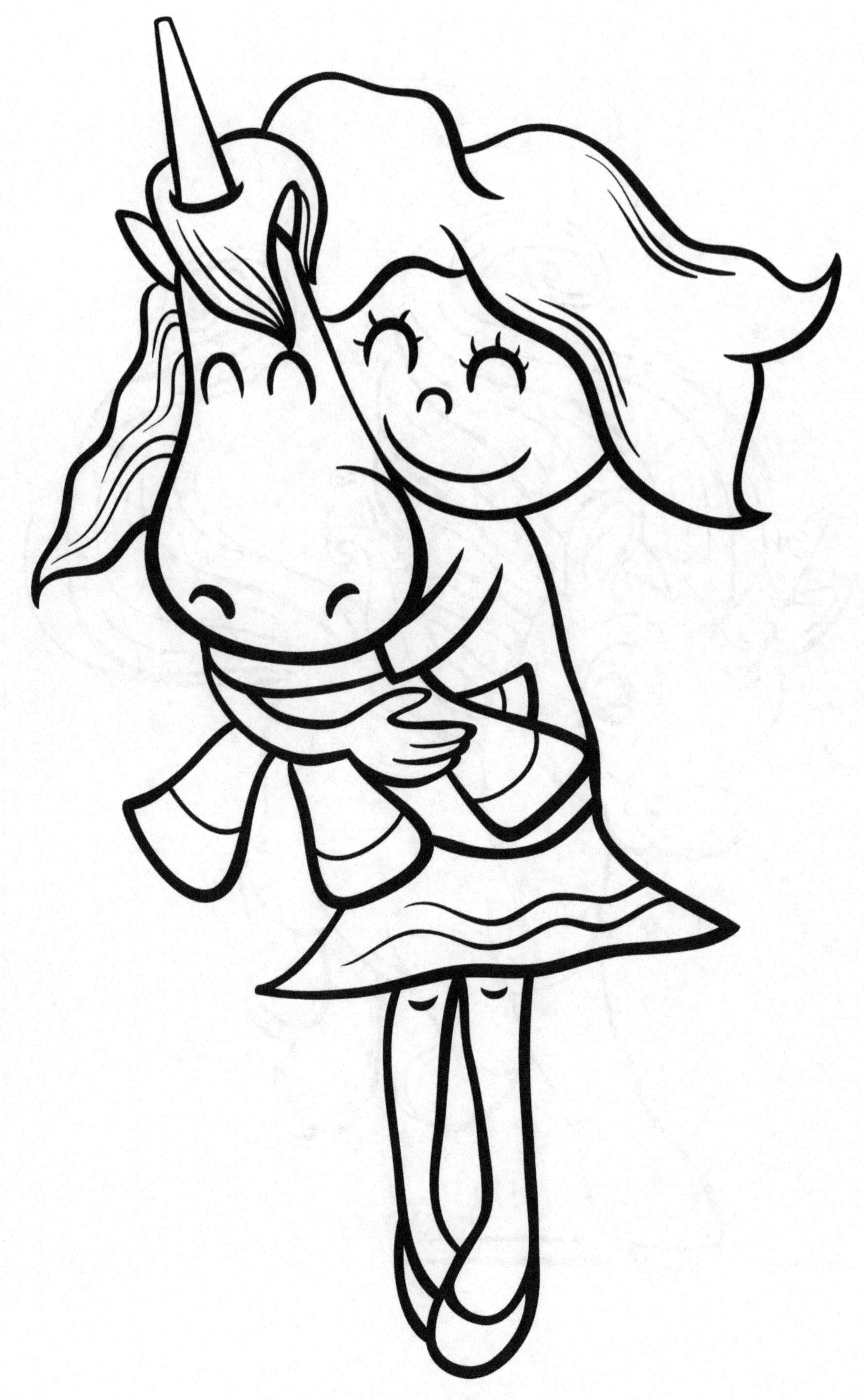

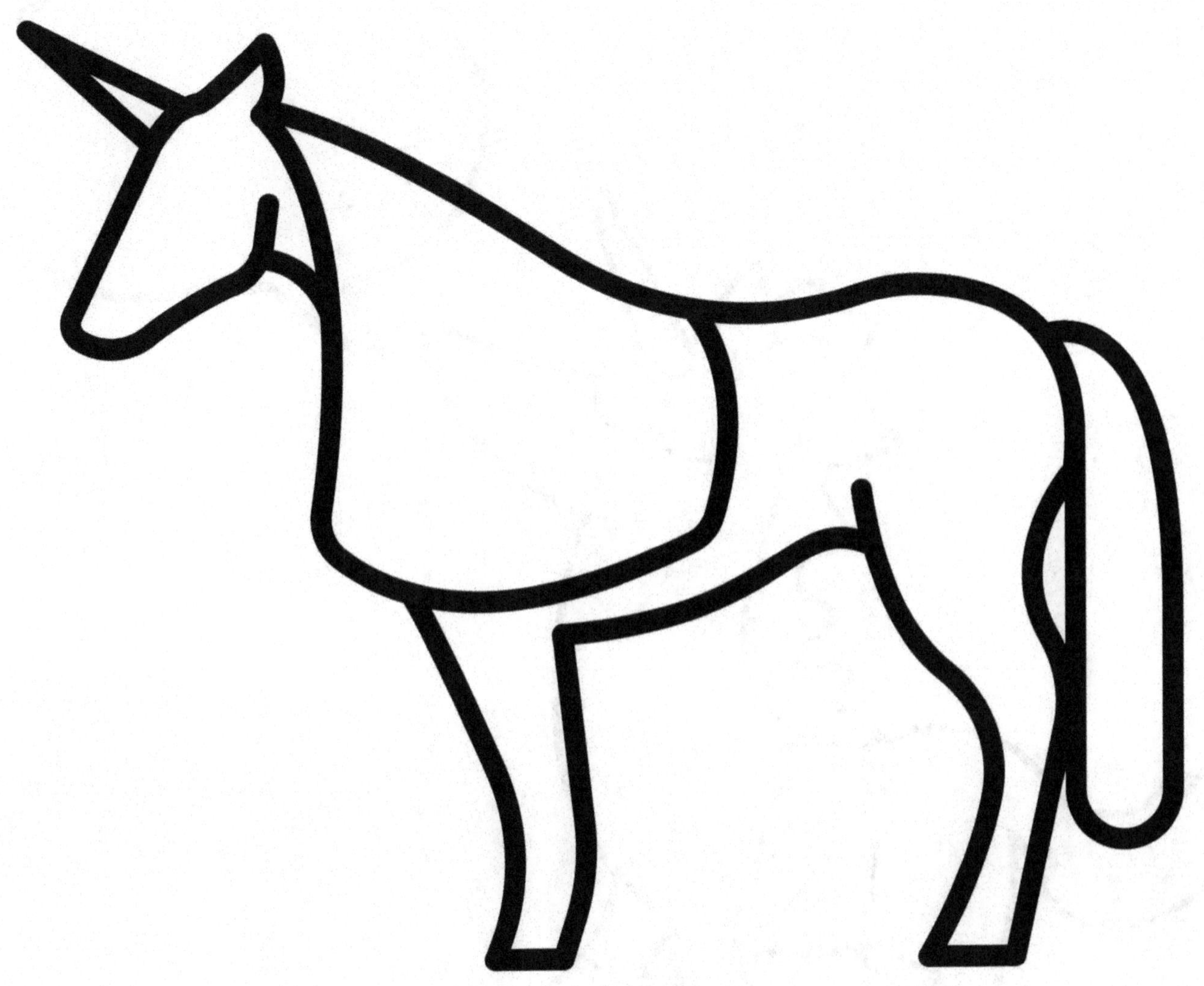

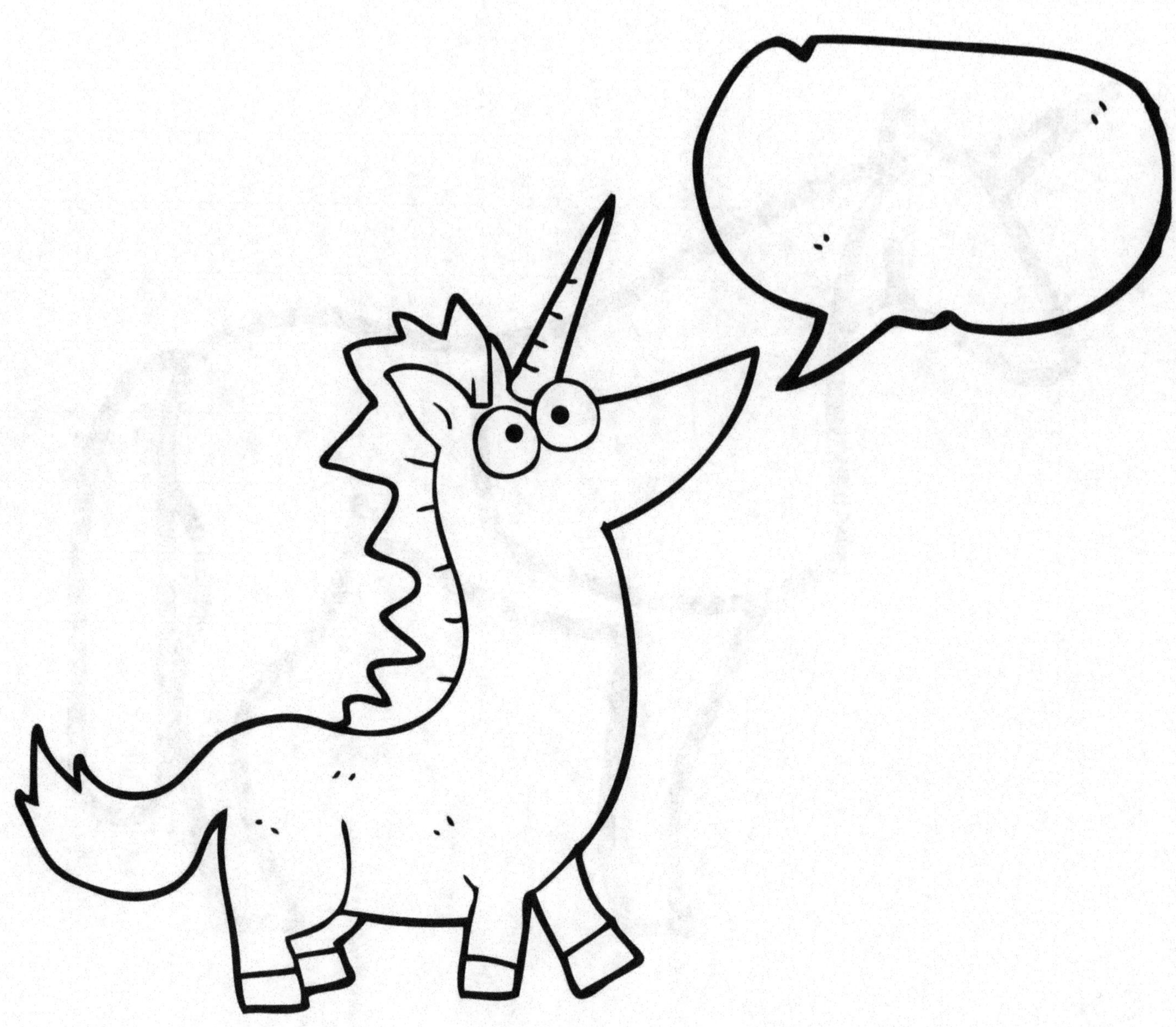

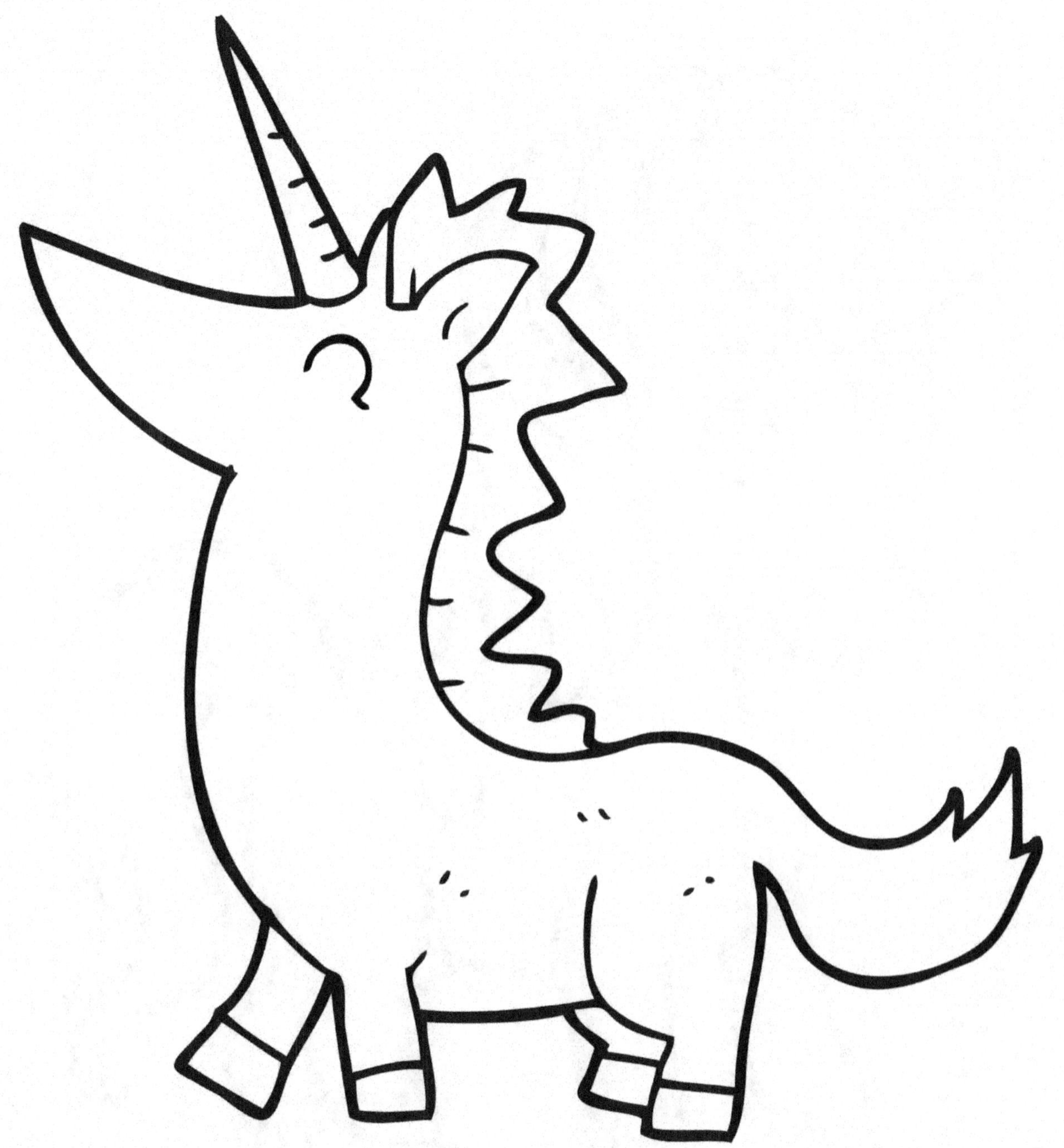

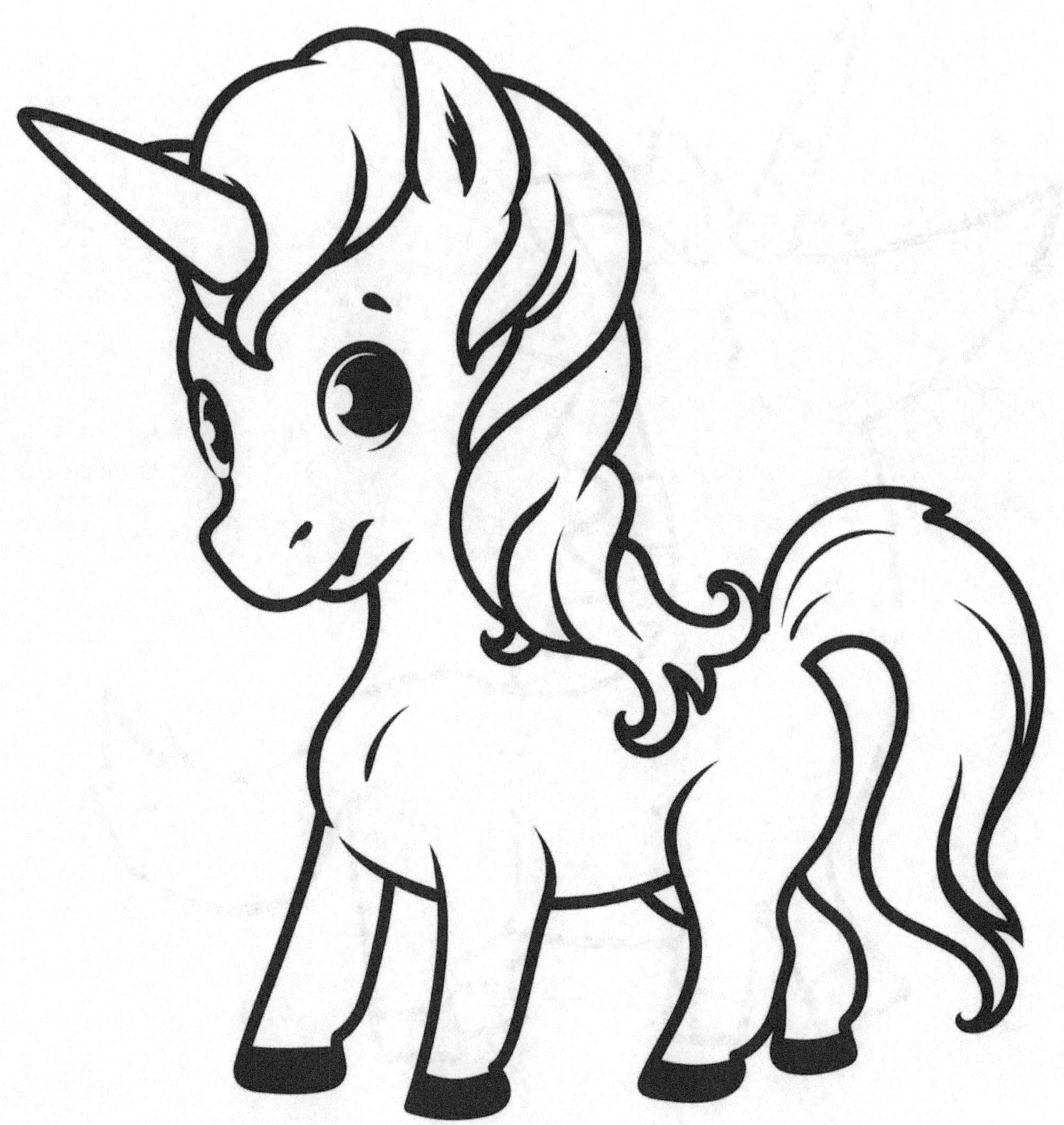

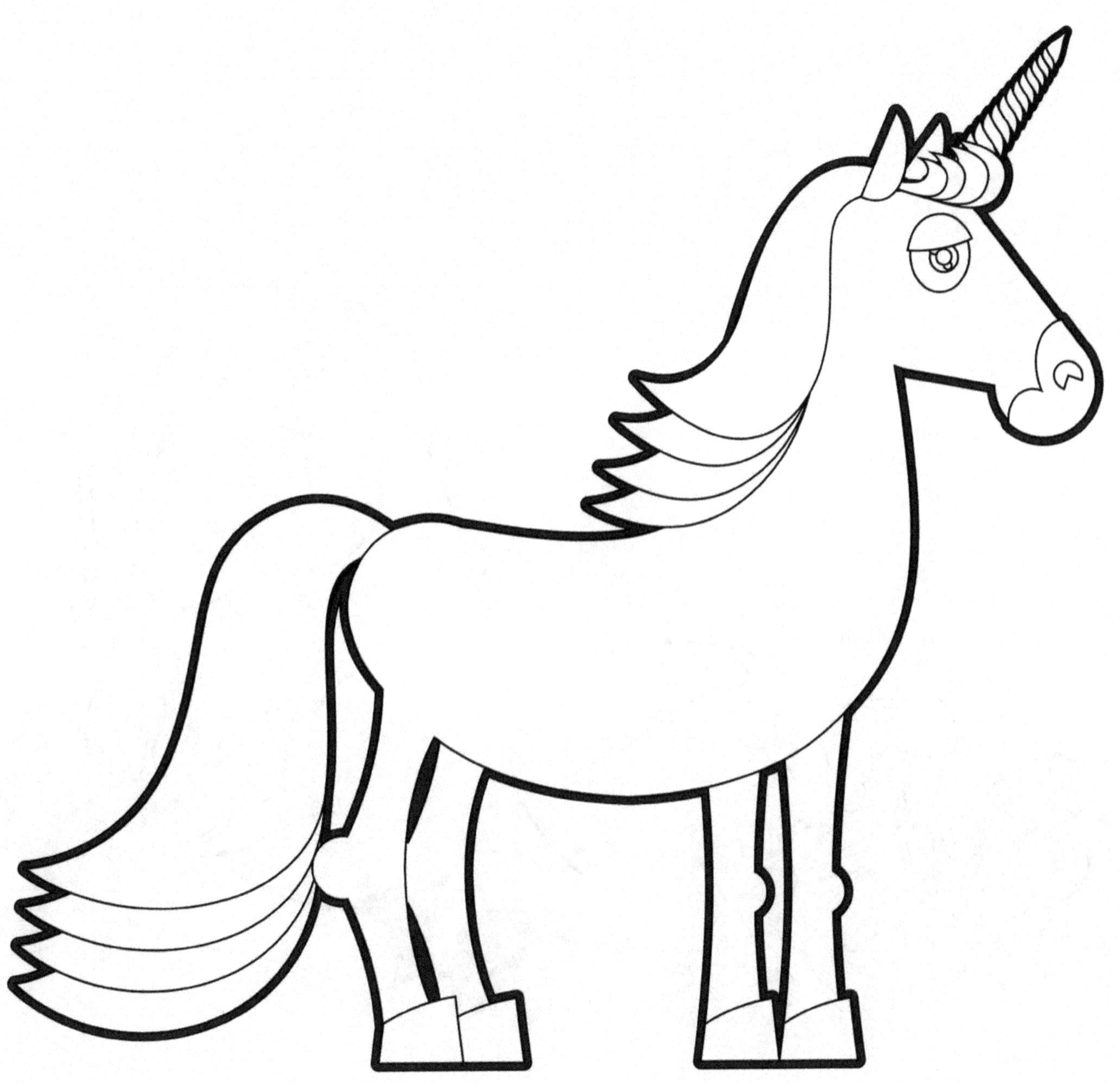

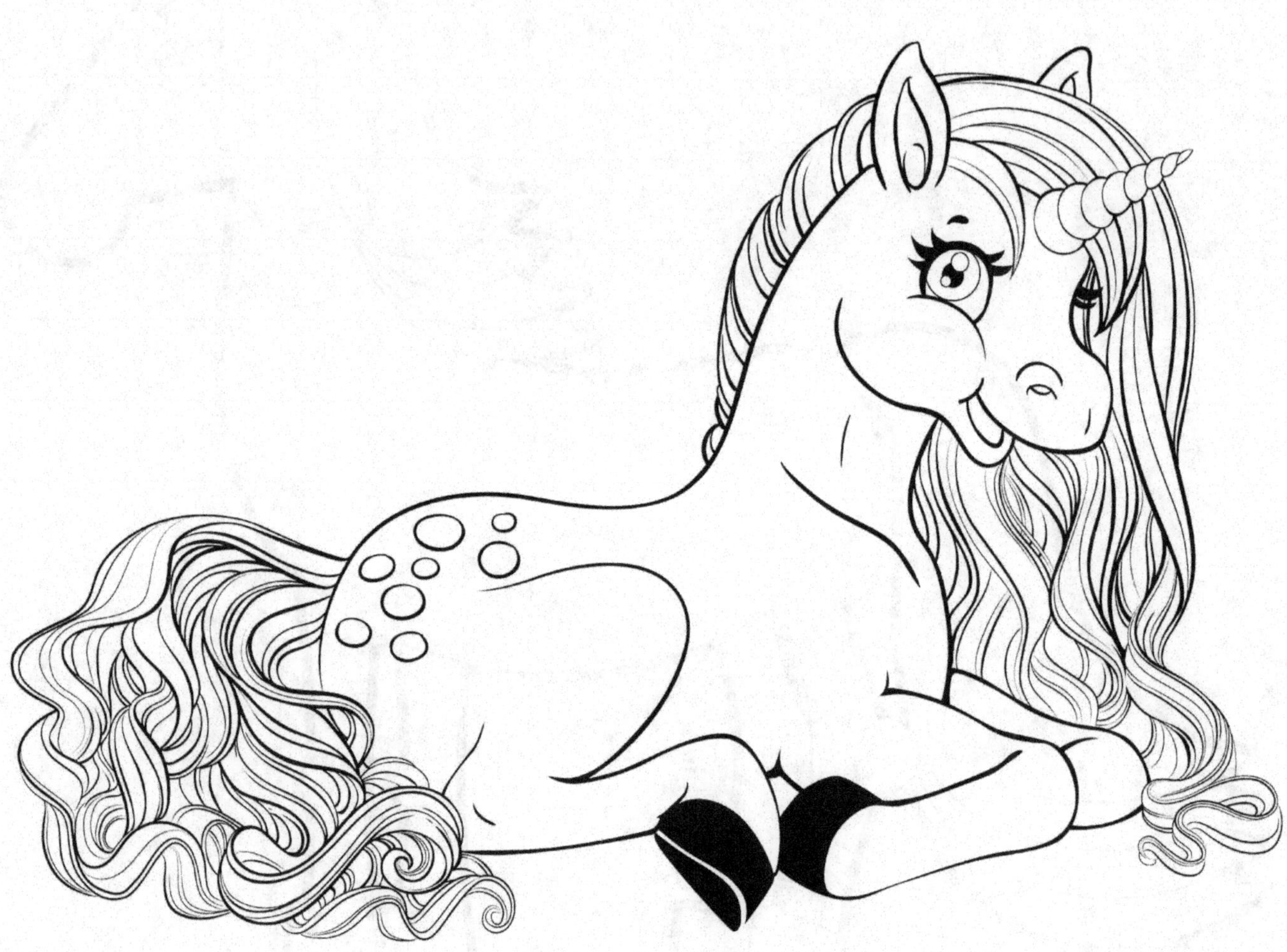

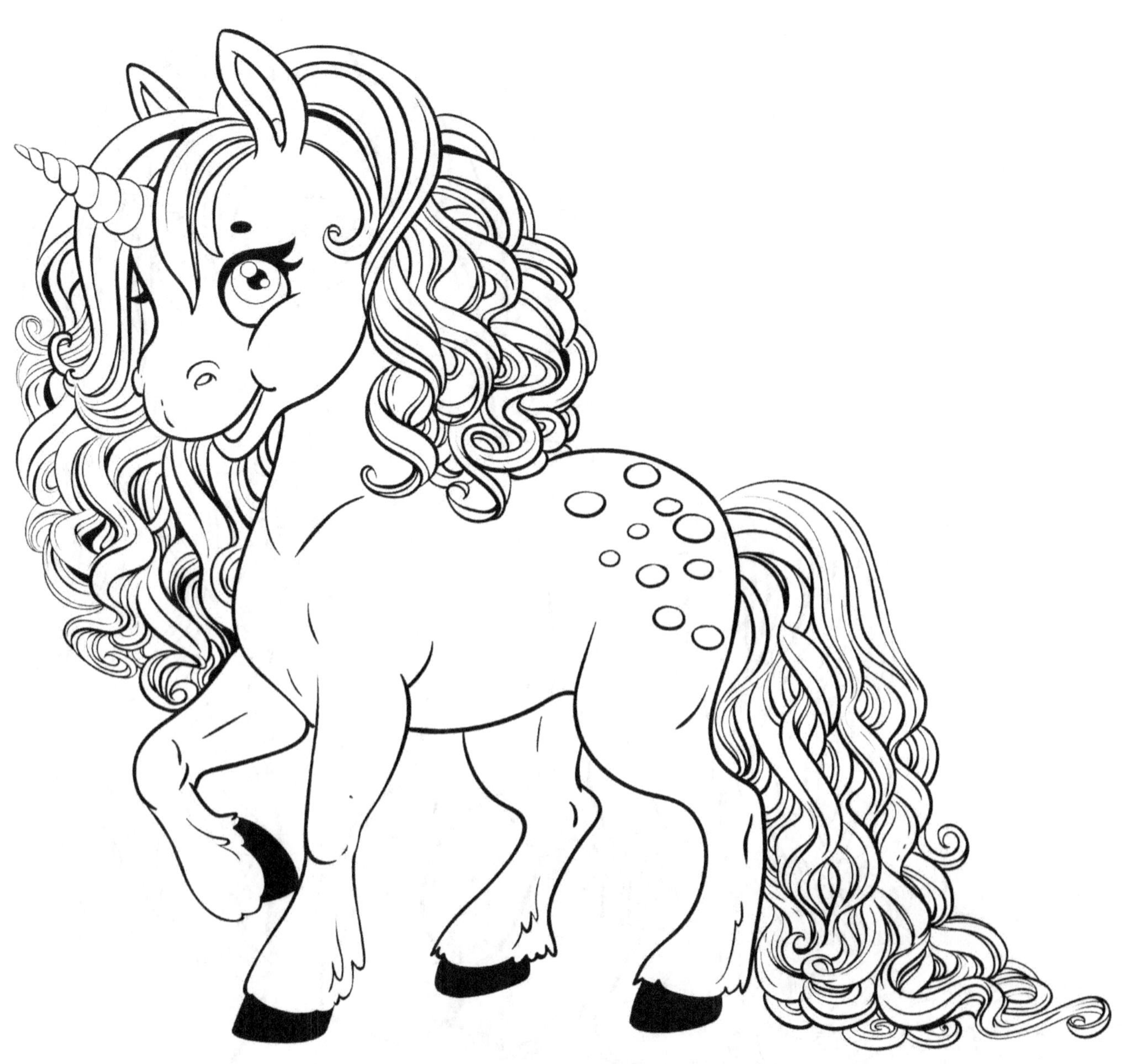

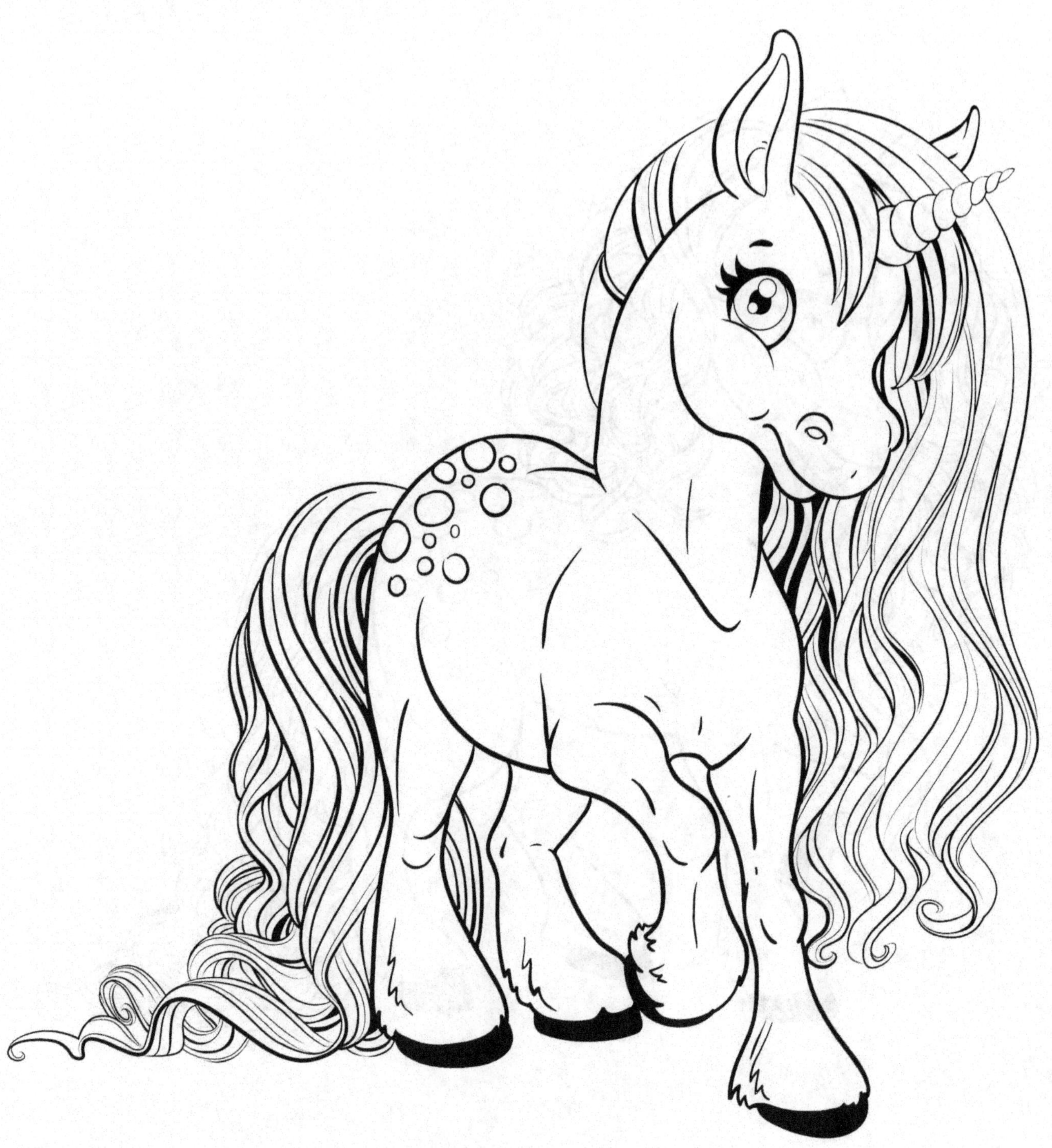

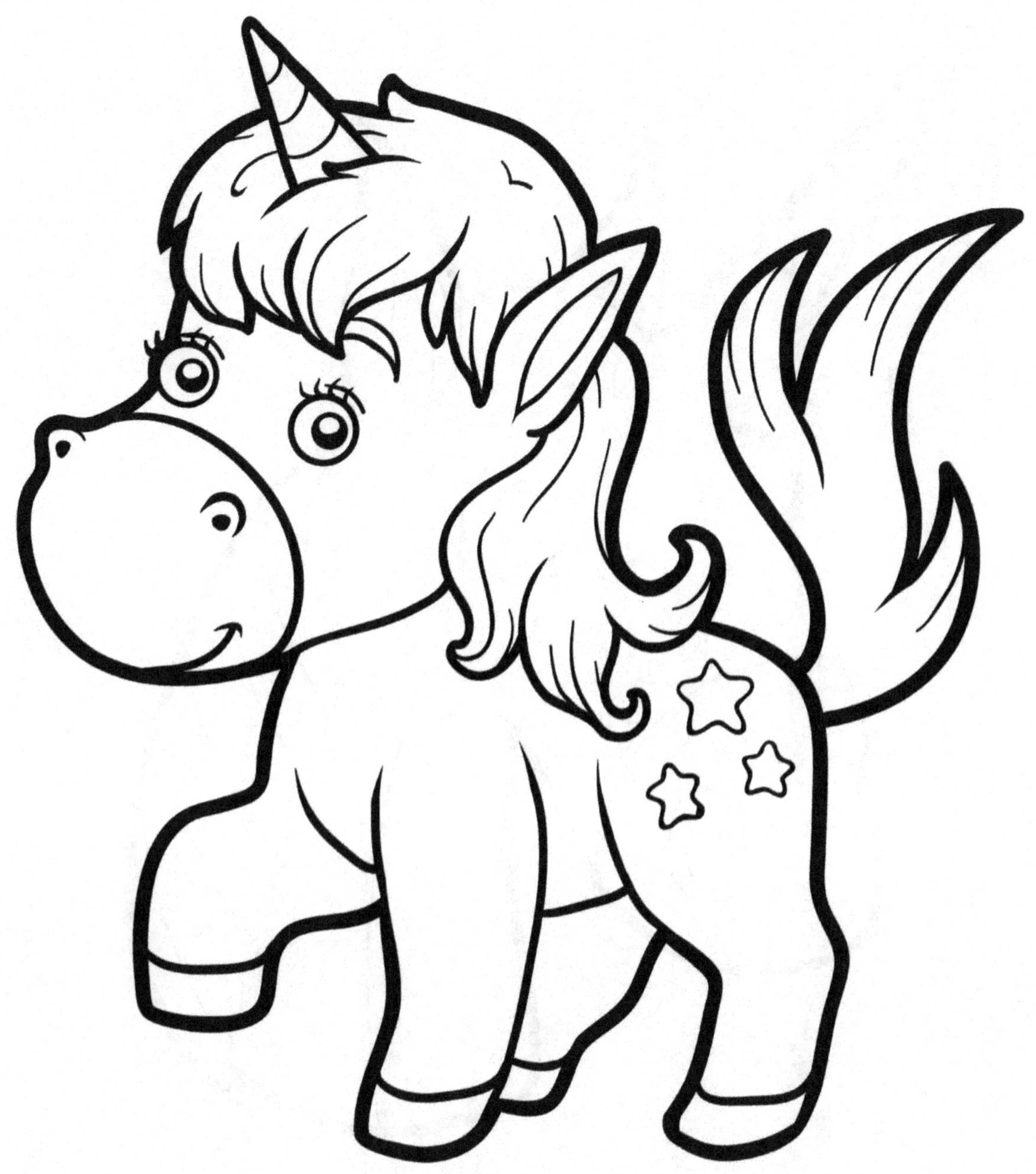

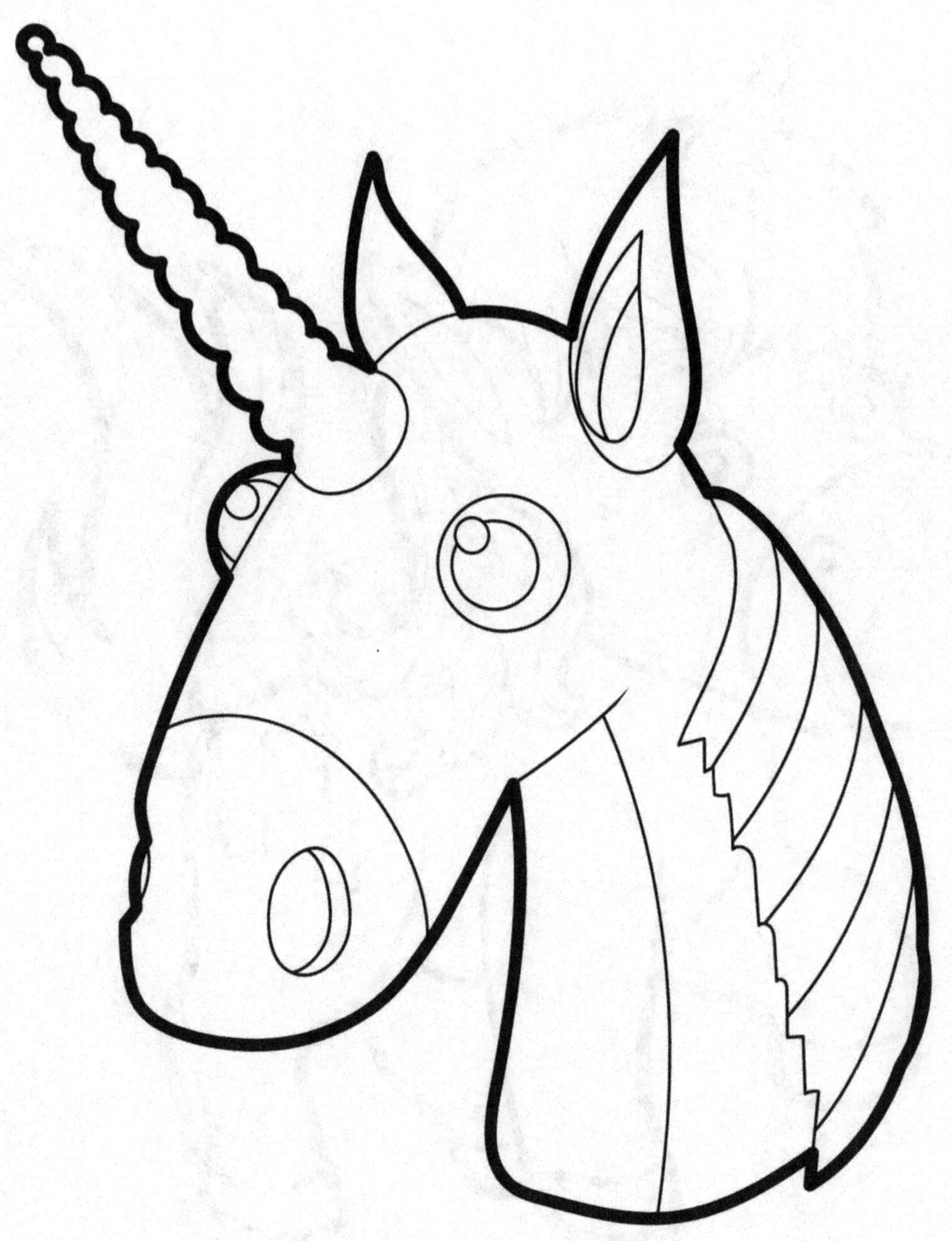

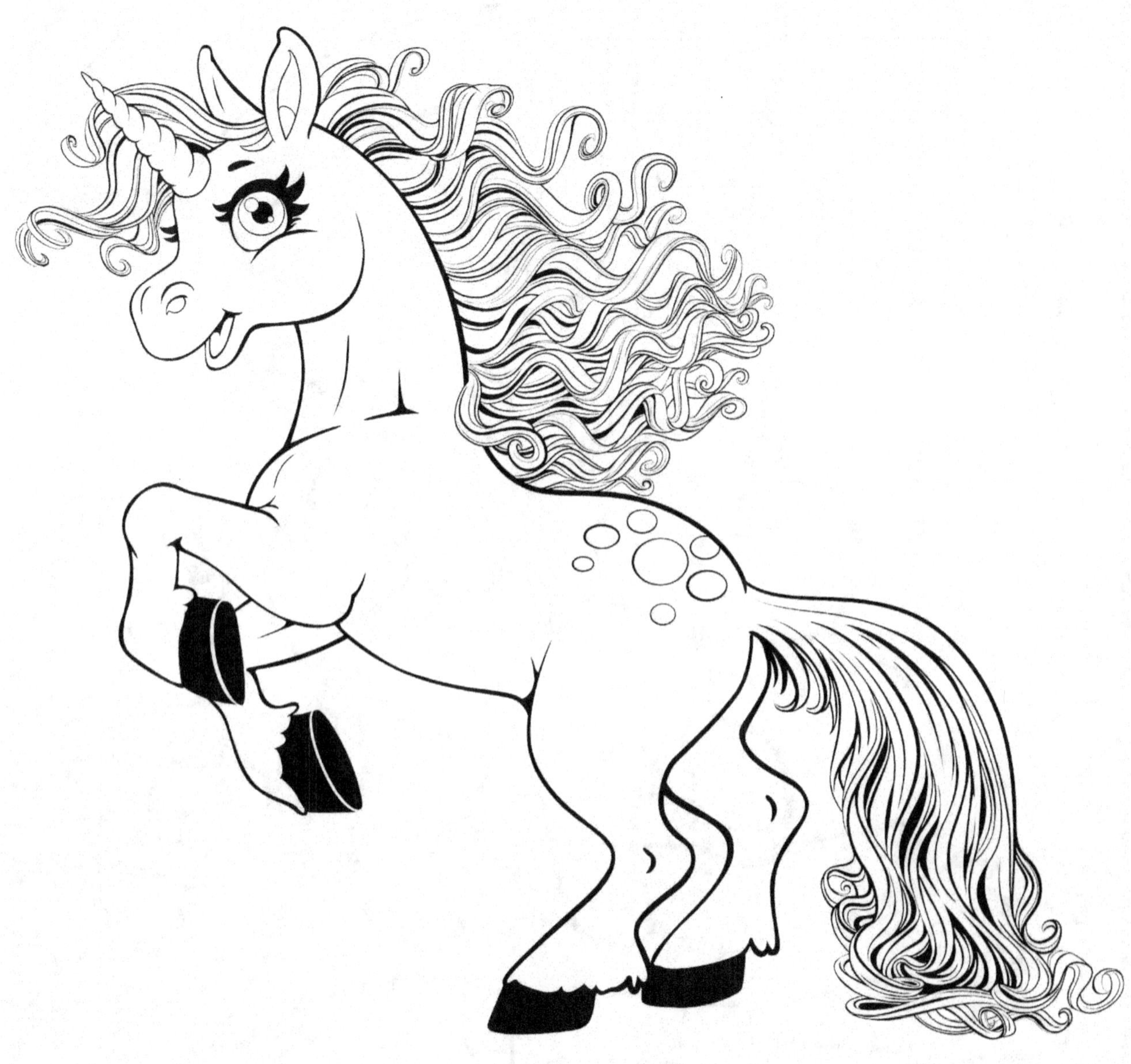

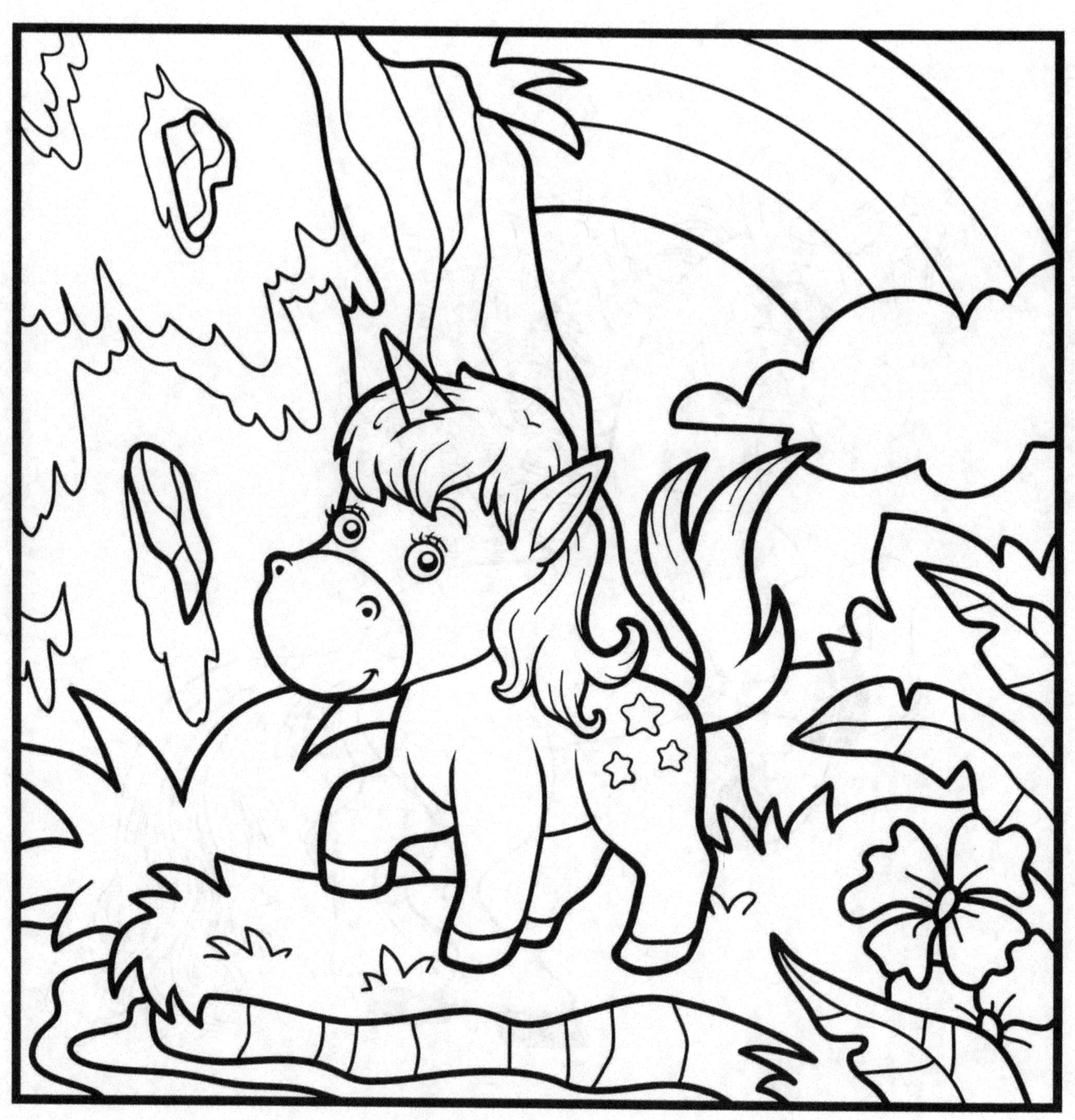

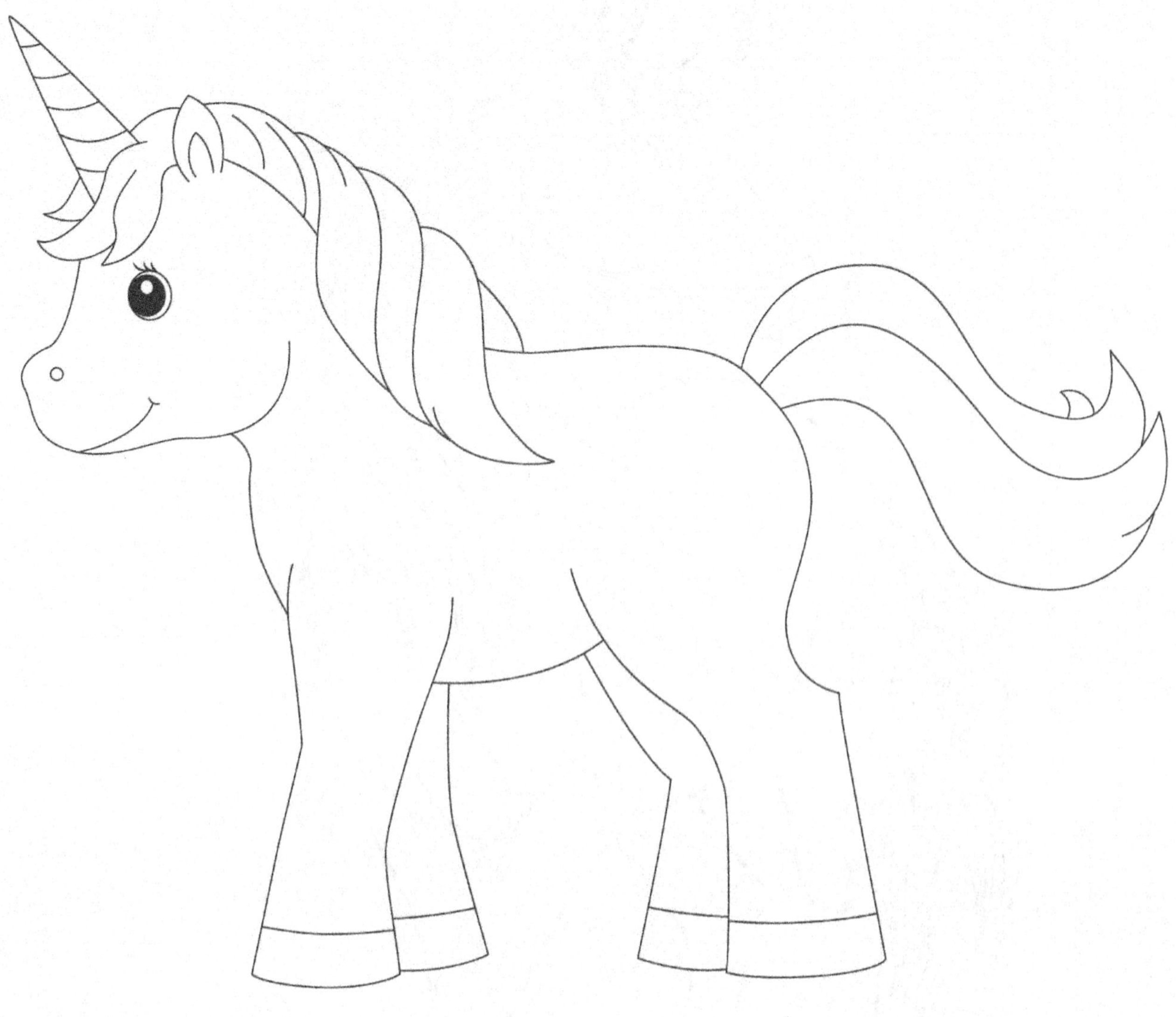

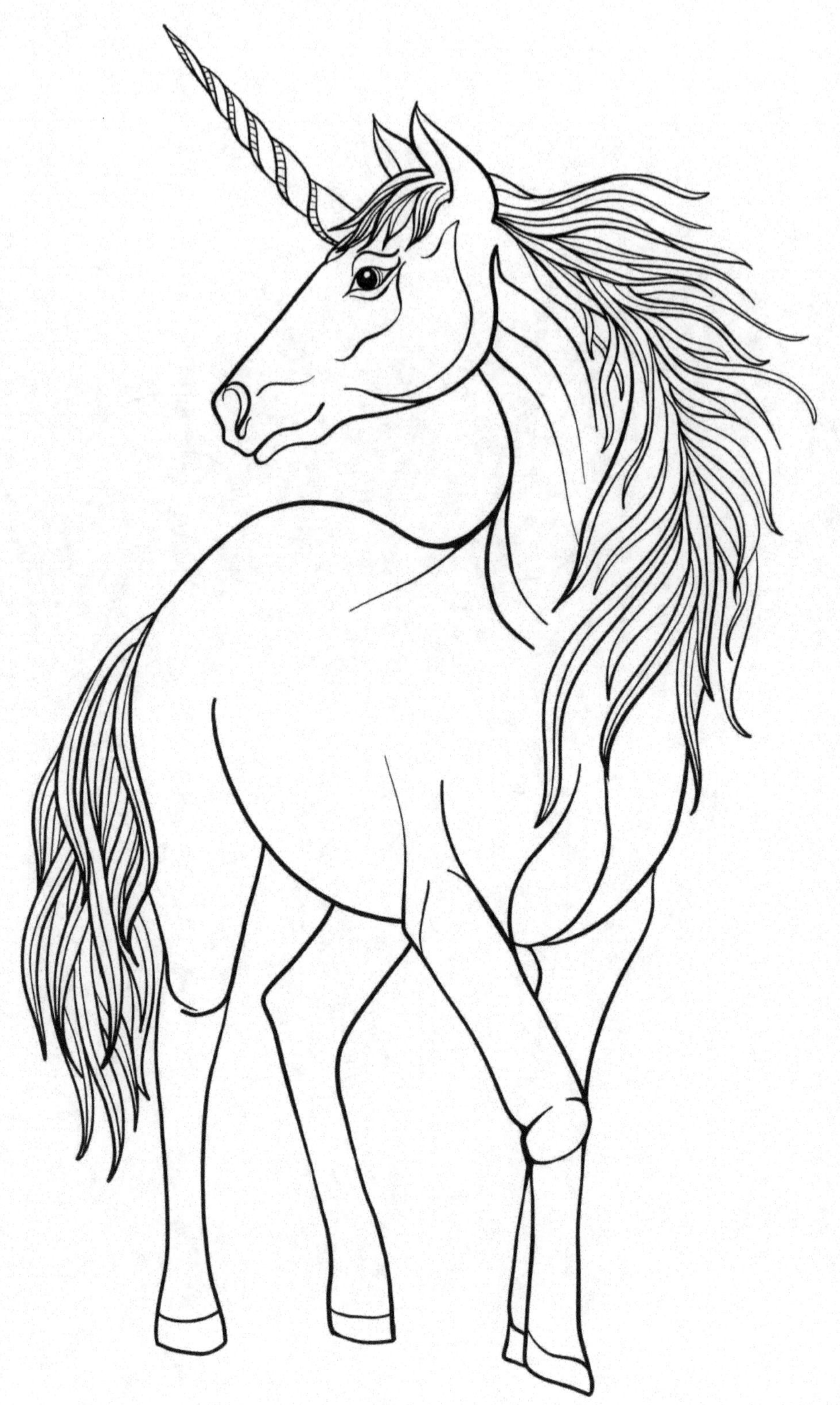

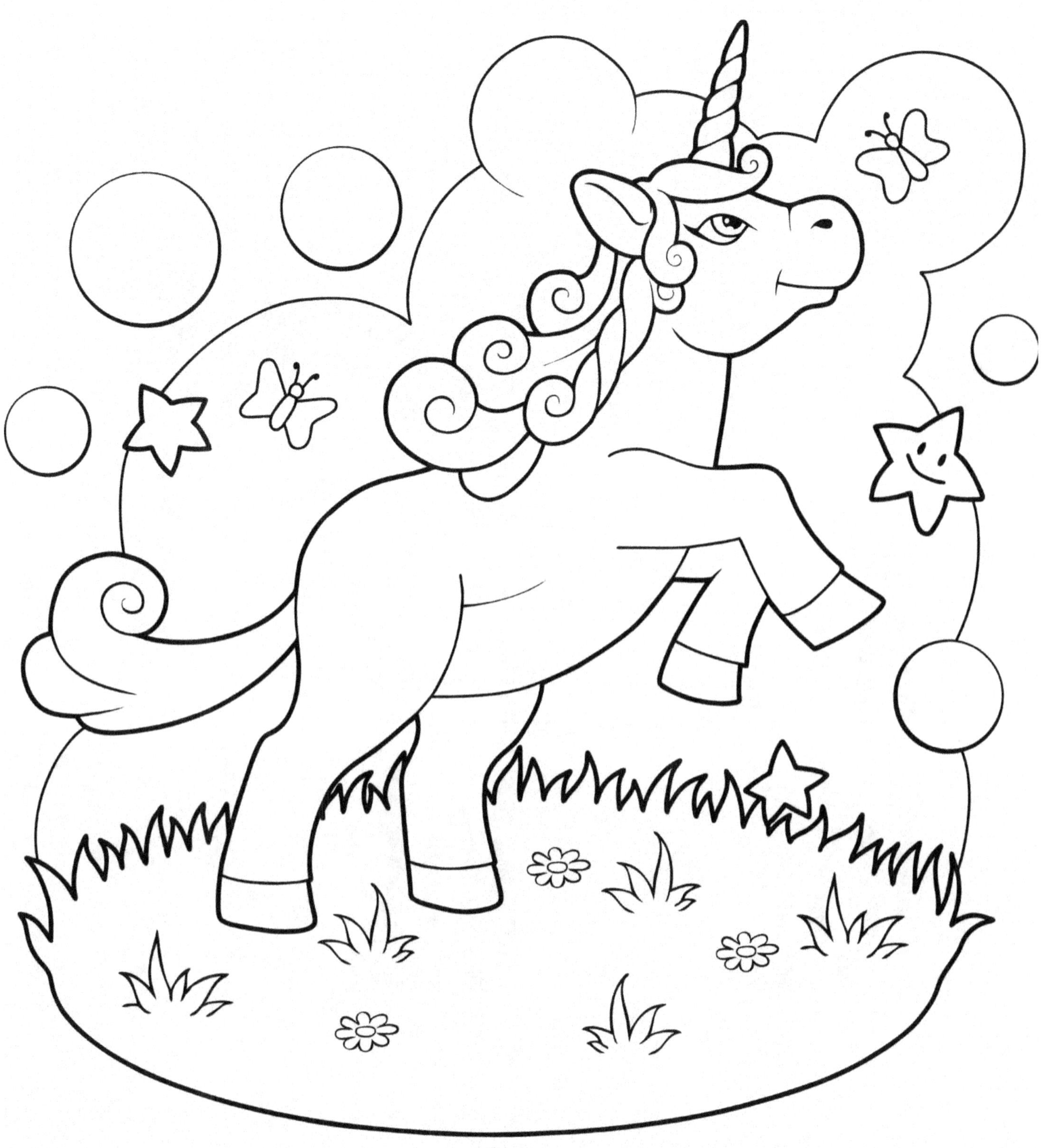

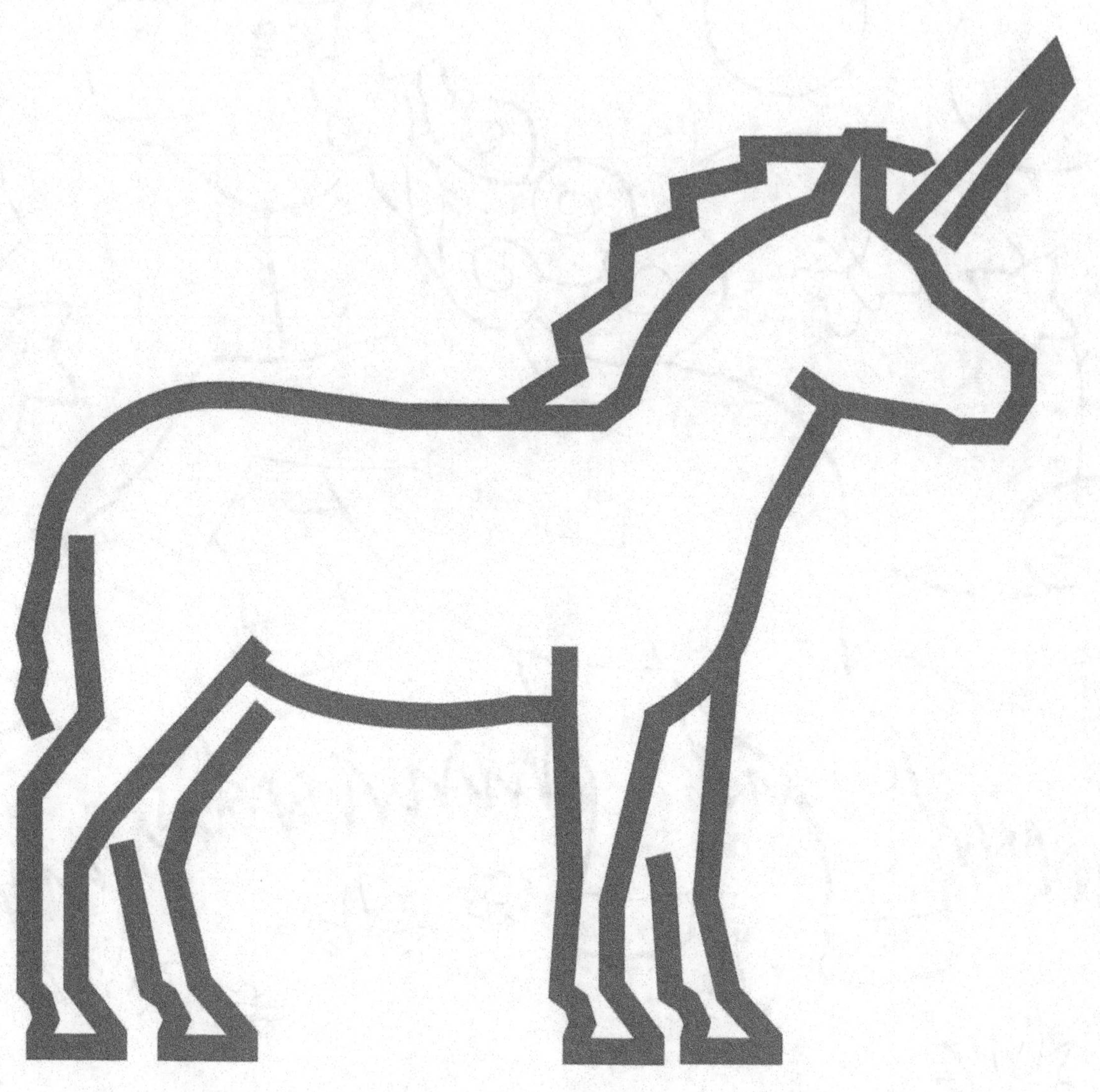

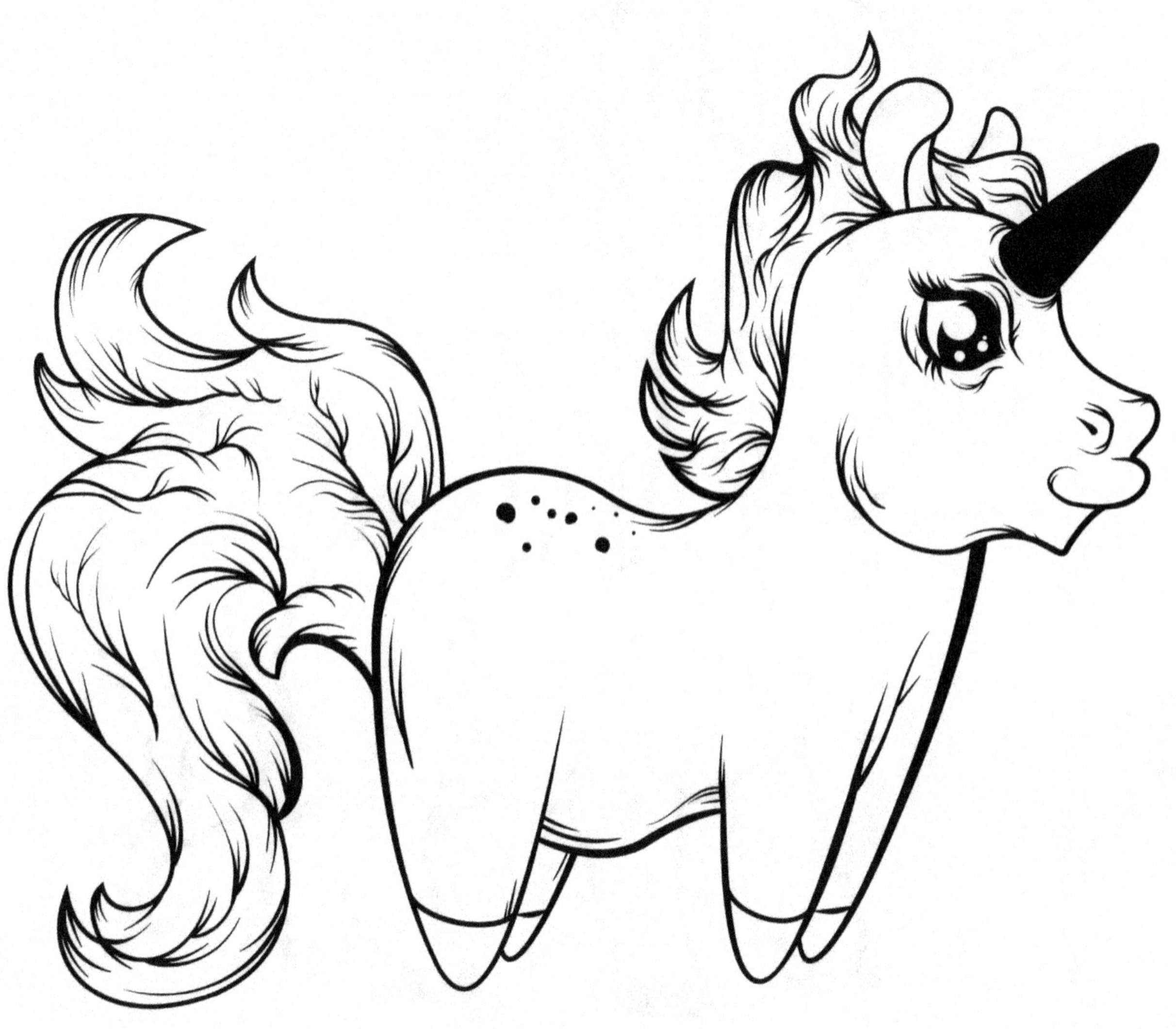

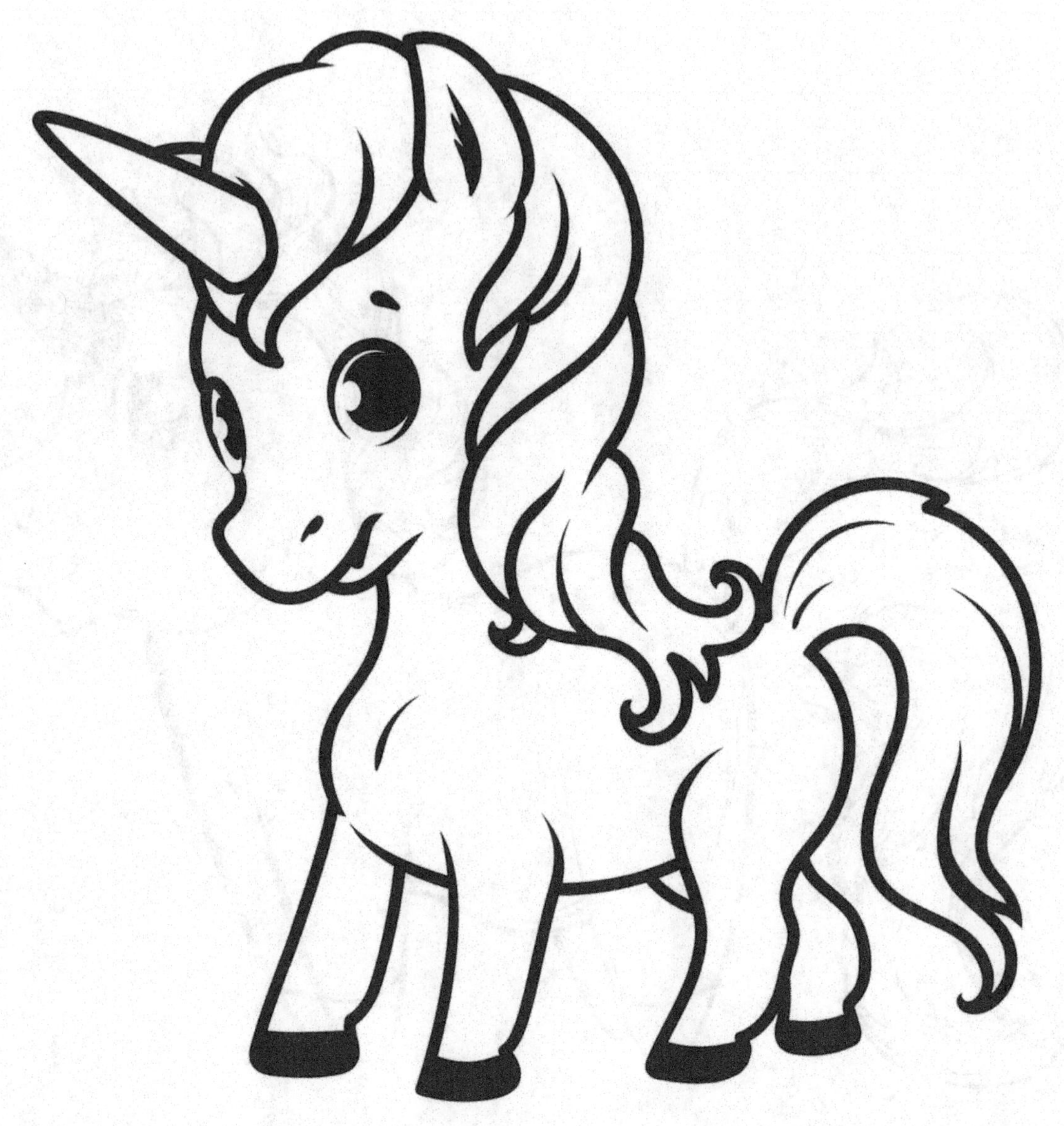